Published by

The Naval & Military Press Ltd
Unit 5 Riverside, Brambleside
Bellbrook Industrial Estate
Uckfield, East Sussex
TN22 1QQ England

Tel: +44 (0)1825 749494

www.naval-military-press.com
www.nmarchive.com

Type.	A. How Recognised when issued.	B. Description.	C. Type of Fuse and Ignition.	D. When, Where and How Grenade should be used.
1 No. 36 Mills Grenade (Hand and Cup Discharger).	Live: Dark Brown, Black in colour. Varnished. Red and/or Green marks top of body. Practice: Gray-White.	Barrel shaped. Serrated to assist fragmentation on explosion. Weight 1¾ lbs. Gas Check must be screwed into Base before use in Cup Discharger.	TIME. .22 Rim Fire Cap. 4-second Fuse, White (Hand thrown). 7-second Fuse, Buff (Cup Discharger, etc.). Filled Baratol.	Anti-Personnel. From cover. Generally bowled over-arm. Clearing Buildings, Trenches, M.G. Nests, etc. Fire from Discharger Cup at 45°, using Ballistite Cartridge only. Recoil considerable.
2 No. 36. Fired from Northover with gas check (if E.Y. Cup Discharger not available).	As above—see 1A.	As above—see 1 B.	As above—see 1 C. 7-second Fuse, but tests have proved that 4-second Fuse can be used.	As above—see 1 D. Propellant—5 drams Powder. Remove Rubber Shock Pad from Propellant.
3 No. 68. Anti-Tank Rifle Grenade Issued completely armed. Must not be Stripped.	Painted Buff, with Red and Green Band round body. Practice: White.	Tail Unit screws into the Body. Tail Unit has a central Sleeve and Four Vanes. Fixed Gas Check. Weight 1½ lbs.	Detonates on impact. (Percussion).	Fired from Discharger (Ballistite Cartridge only) against all armoured fighting vehicles, lorries, etc. Some forms of Demolition. Propellant—30 grain Ballistite Cartridge, half the length of which is black. Recoil considerable.
4 No. 69. Bakelite Hand Grenade issued complete except for priming. Must not be stripped.	Black Bakelite. Red Band or X's round top of body. Practice: White.	Barrel shape. Similar to 36 M. Weight approximately 1 lb.	All-ways. Instantaneous. Detonates on impact. (Percussion). Amatol or Lyddite.	Anti-Personnel (Blast). Morale generally. Confined spaces best effects. Useful in dry weather for making dust cloud if smoke not available. Can be thrown any method as situation demands. Can be used under certain conditions as "Aid to Realism" in exercises and battle practice.

E. Range and Danger Area.	F. Type of Effects.	G. To Prepare and Prime.	H. Mechanism in Operation.
Hand, 25-35 yards. (Can inflict wounds up to 100 yards.) Cup Discharger, Gas Port fully open, 80 yds. at 45°. Gas Port fully closed, 200 yds. at 45°.	Anti-Personnel. Fragments in all directions parallel to ground and upwards. Shrapnel effects can be obtained if thrown to burst about 6 feet or more above objective. Ditto Cup Discharger.	Remove Base Plug, clean and insert Igniter Set. Replace Base Plug. Attach Gas Check for E.Y. Cup.	Withdrawal of Safety Pin leaves hand (or Cup Discharger) in control of Lever. When Grenade is thrown or fired, Lever flies off and releases Striker, which is forced on to Cap of Igniter Set by the Spring, and ignites Fuse. Keep Lever in palm of hand. The Fuse burns for four seconds (7 seconds E.Y. Cup). Explodes Detonator which explodes Grenade.
As above—see 1 E. 75-150 yards.	As above—see 1 F. But Shrapnel effects easier to obtain.	As above—see 1 G. But Northover.	As above—see 1 H. But read "Breech" instead of Discharger.
50-100 yards. Special Sight. Gas Port on Discharger fully closed always. Recoil considerable. Use from Northover in emergency only. Only direct hits are effective with careful sighting. Accuracy is most reliable.	Penetration. On impact will perforate armour of light, medium, and sometimes parts of heavy Tanks. The force of the explosion is in a restricted forward direction.	Primed and Detonated Ready.	Pull out Safety Pin, place Grenade (Fins and Gas Check first) into Cup, withdraw Safety Pin. Shear Wire breaks on firing, leaving Striker free. (Shear Wire generally does not break when fired from Northover, but Grenade will explode if direct hit registered with sufficient force).
Generally up to 50 yards. Hand only. Small Radius, approx. 10 yards. In Practice all " Blinds," must be found and destroyed, as will explode if trodden on.	Blast. Lethal under some conditions. Momentary Shock. Morale.	Remove Base Plug. Insert Detonator open end first.	Remove Safety Cap, Safety Tape being held in position by thumb and finger of throwing hand. When thrown, Safety Bolt on Tape falls out and upon impact Creep Spring is overcome, the Striker fires the Cap and explodes the Detonator, which in turn explodes the Grenade. Designed to explode on impact of any part of the exterior of this Grenade.

See Sketch A.

See Sketch B.

See Sketch C.

Type.	A. How Recognised when issued.	B. Description.	C. Type of Fuse and Ignition.	D. When, Where and How Grenade should be used.
5 No. 73. A.T. Grenade.	Painted Buff with Red Band, and Stencilled 73 A.T. Practice : White.	Cylindrical. 10 ins. high, 3 ins. diameter (Thermos Flask). Weight 4 lbs. approx.	All-ways Instantaneous. (Percussion). Gelignite, 3½ lbs. approximately.	Against all Lorries, etc. Can also be used in numbers as Mines, etc., in street fighting, with correct Fusing. Above from Buildings. Generally thrown over-arm, held with fingers passing either side of safety tape.
6 No. 74. S.T. Hand Grenade (Sticky).	Ball shaped, about five inches in diameter. Enclosed in Khaki painted Tin Outer Casing. Black Bakelite Handle. Practice : Wood Model, painted white, with steel band for correct weight.	Glass Flask. Filled with H.E. Protected by Metal Khaki Casing which is removed before using Grenade. Flask is covered by a sticky envelope. Inside neck of Flask is a Tube to hold a Detonator Assembly. A Black Bakelite Handle with a No. 36 type Striker is fitted. Weight 2½ lbs. approximately.	1½ lbs. Nitro-Glycerine in Glass Flask ; covered with Bird Lime. 5-second Fuse. Detonator and C.E. Pellet.	Against all A.F.V.'s, etc. Designed to stick to its Target. Will not adhere to a wet or muddy surface. Can be thrown from upper floor windows on to Tanks, etc., with good effect. Can also be placed on Target by hand, but cover must be taken before Grenade explodes, i.e., under five seconds. Also useful for demolition work in street fighting.
7 No. 75 & 75a. Known as the Hawkins Grenade or Grenade Mine.	Buff in colour with 75 or 75a painted on Striker Plate. Those marked 75 contain 100% explosive. 75a has 80% explosive. Practice : Dull Red.	Is a Talcum Powder Tin fitted with a Metal Striker Plate or Platform on one side. Weight about 2½ lbs.	Instantaneous. Explodes when crushed. (Minimum crushing weight about 2 cwts.). The Detonator Unit consists of an Igniter and Detonator. Two used with each Grenade. The Igniter is a Tin Plate Tube closed at one end by flattening, and is painted Red. A rubber band is rolled on the Igniter. The Detonator is an Aluminium Tube open at one end and smaller in diameter than Igniter. It must be handled carefully. 1½ lbs. approx. Ammonal and 4 ozs. Victor Powder.	To be placed in the pathway of an oncoming A.F.V. and can be used to form a mine field. Placed up to and within 2 ft. of each other, sympathetic explosion results. "Necklace" best used in contacting A.F.V. tracks or tyres.
8 No. 76. S.I.P. (Self-Igniting Phosphorus).	Half Pint Clear Glass Bottle. Red Cap Hand, Green Cap Hand or "North-over."		Instantaneous on breaking. (Percussion). Yellow Phosphorus, Benzene, Rubber and Water.	A.F.V.'s, Lorries, etc., and all forms of Incendiarism.

E. Range and Danger Area.	F. Type of Effects.	G. To Prepare and Prime.	H. Mechanism in Operation.	
Hand only, 12-15 yards. Thrower must have adequate cover owing to terrific blast.	Morale and Blast effect is great. Material effect is considerable on objects at point of burst.	Remove Lid, Insert Detonator closed end first.	Remove Safety Cap of All-ways Fuse. Tape and Pin will fall out during flight, leaving Striker free to overcome Creep Spring on impact. Designed to burst from any point of impact.	See Sketch D.
Approx. 20 yards, hand thrown. Blast effect is local and forward unless exploded in mid-air.	Blast lethal and Morale. When sticking to its Target the H.E. has its maximum effect. Will perforate or destroy .nat part of the Target to which it adheres.	Unscrew Neck Ring, remove Plug and insert Detonator Assembly. Screw on Handle. Make sure rubber bands are in correct position on Detonator Set.	Remove outer Casing, pull out Safety Pin with Tag marked "Danger," Lever flies off and releases Striker when thrown. (Make absolutely sure that the small circular knurled brass nut in top of Handle, holding Lever, is firmly in position before pulling out Safety Pin.)	See Sketch E.
Hand only. About 20 yards. Container is light and distintegrates completely. Blast is Heavy. Danger area may be up to 75 yards.	High Blast effect, sideways and upwards.	Insert Igniter and Detonator, square cut end first. Do not remove Cap at end of Body.	The Grenade is shaped so that, when thrown, it will come to rest with the Striker Plate either on top or underneath. It will operate equally well in both positions. Is safe until run over and Striker Plate crushed.	See Sketch F.
Hand, about 20-30 yards. Northover, 75-150 yards. To wherever Liquid splashes.	Incendiary and Smoke.	Ready.	Immediately Dangerous. If used for Incendiary purpose in Blitzed house, should have Detonator and Safety Fuse attached to side of Bottle to ensure breaking.	See Sketch G.

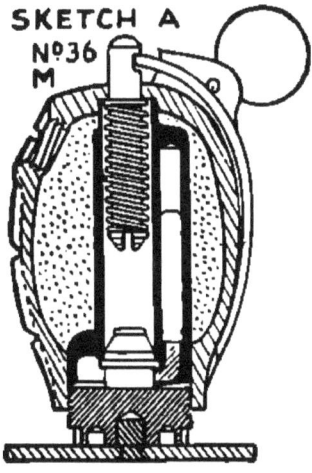

SKETCH A
Nº36
M

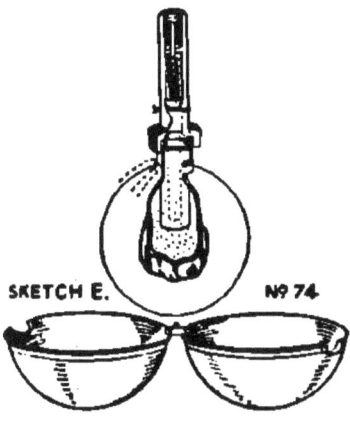

SKETCH E.   Nº 74

Nº 68 A.T.

SKETCH B.

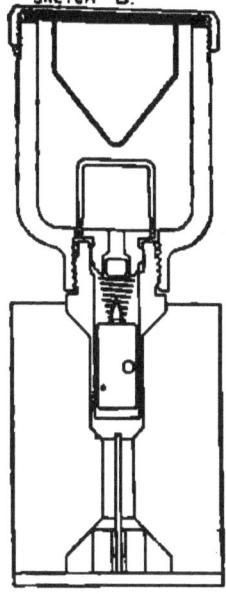

Nº 69

SKETCH C.

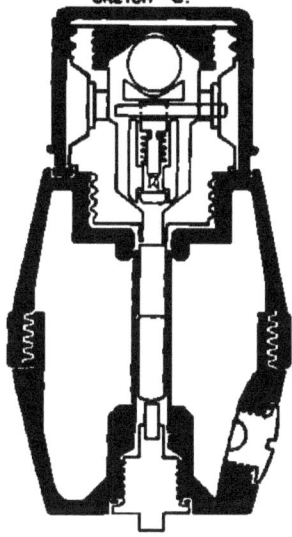

Nº 73 A.T.

SKETCH D.

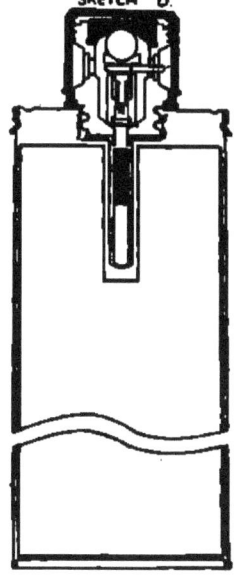

SKETCH F   Nº 75 & 75A

SKETCH G.   Nº 76.

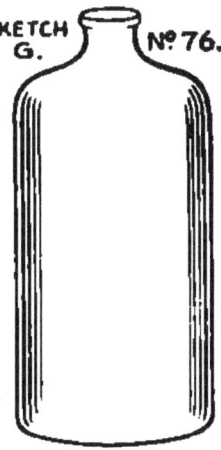

COLT .455 inch, .38 inch and .45 inch REVOLVERS.

DETAILS.—There are many different types of Colt revolvers, making it almost impossible to give full details of each as many vary in small details only, but the following main particulars will be all that will be needed in order to use the weapon.

The cylinder turns clockwise and has 6 chambers. The ammunition, which can be used for the different calibres, is as follows :—

The .45 inch uses any American .45 inch revolver ammunition.

The .38 inch, as long as the cylinder is over $1\frac{1}{2}$ inches in length, will use any .38 inch American revolver ammunition.

The .455 inch will use any American or British .455 inch ammunition.

The .38 inch, when the cylinder is less than $1\frac{1}{2}$ inches in length, will only use .38 inch Colt short type ammunition or the standard British service .38 inch ammunition.

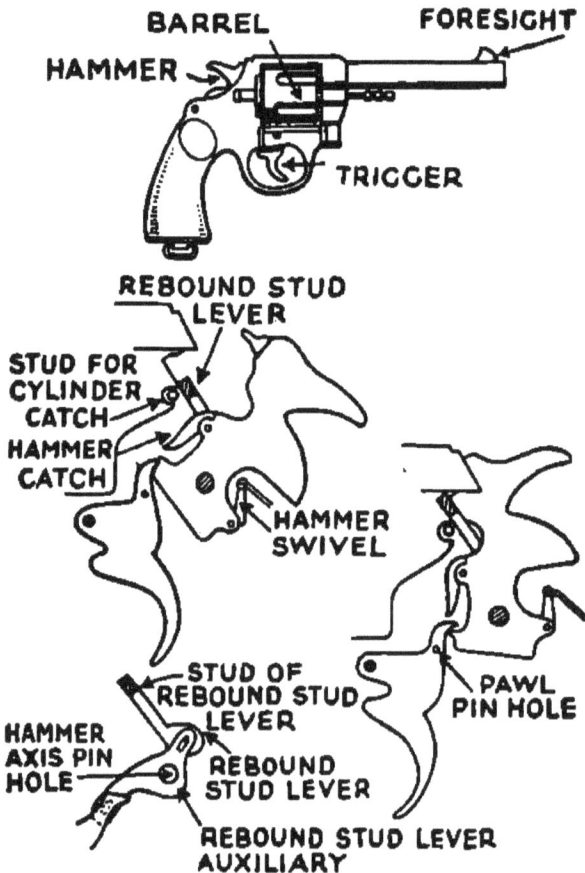

·455 COLT REVOLVER WITH FULL MECHANISM

STRIPPING.—Undo screw holding butt grips. Undo side plate to screws which is on the left hand side of the pistol, then prise up the left side plate by means of a knife fitted under the plate in between the two arms of the lock spring and take off complete with nose piece and cylinder cap. This causes all the actual mechanism to be fully open. Then remove the remaining parts in the following order : Take out pawl and, by means of a punch, hammer out mainspring auxiliary axis pin and remove the auxiliary.

Next, by means of pincers, grip together the long and short arms of the mainspring and manipulate the mainspring out—at the same time undoing its claws from the hammer swivel arms. Turn the hammer rearwards until its nose is clear of the body and then take out. Push trigger to the fore, pull cylinder catch stud backwards and take out. Take out trigger with rebound stud lever and rebound stud lever auxiliary. Finally, undo cylinder stop screw on the right side of the body over the trigger guard and take out cylinder to the front.

ASSEMBLY.—Refit cylinder spring stop and screw. Replace the rebound stud lever auxiliary, rebound stud lever and trigger in one unit, seeing that the pins of the rebound stud lever and the trigger are in their correct recesses in the rebound stud lever auxiliary. Fit cylinder catch stud and, by holding trigger backwards, refit hammer. Then refit axis pin and mainspring auxiliary. The mainspring is refitted by compressing it as is done when stripping. Engage the claws on the hammer swivel arms and fit the spring short arm over the top of the mainspring auxiliary, then fit the mainspring stem into its bed. See that the trigger is then forward so that the mainspring auxiliary lies over the pawl pin. Refit pawl by placing its pin in the trigger nose hole. Finally lift up the nose of the mainspring auxiliary so that the pawl can be pushed right down home. Replace side plate, at the same time pressing thumb piece to the rear until the stud and cylinder catch engage, then refit screws in the side plate and replace butt grips.

It should be noted that, after each component part is fitted, care should be taken to see that it functions in a correct mechanical manner.

MECHANISM.—The cylinder is held in the firing position due to the cylinder catch stud being held fully home in its recess in the middle of the back of the cylinder due to the cylinder catch stud spring. Should the cylinder not completely engage it is impossible for the hammer and trigger to be operated because the extractor has pushed to the rear the cylinder catch thumb piece which, in turn, pulls the cylinder catch stud far enough to the back to interfere with the normal relowering movement of the rebound stud lever. Finally hammer rebound by the shoulder of the mainspring lever which is after pressed down by the mainspring, touches the back face of the hammer tail and presses it to the fore. This forces the hammer to turn on its axis pin so that the hammer nose is pressed back. Mechanical safety is effected by the hammer tail back face pressing against the mainspring lever safety face and, after rebound, this prevents the hammer nose from making contact with the cap of the round of ammunition. When the trigger is pulled to the back this causes the rebound stud lever stud to drop behind the cylinder catch stud and, therefore, the cylinder is locked in the firing position. Should it not lock then the trigger cannot be pulled completely to the back because the rebound stud lever stud will not clear the cylinder catch stud, which is in a protuberant position due to the fact that it cannot be pressed fully home in its bed in the cylinder.

COLT .455 inch and .45 inch
AUTOMATIC PISTOLS.

DETAILS.—Total length, approximately 8 inches. Barrel length, 4¾ inches, including the chamber. Weighs 2¾ lbs. loaded, 2 lbs. 6 ozs. unloaded. Holds 7 rounds. Ammunition used is .455 inch and .45 inch rimless pattern automatic ammunition. NOTE CAREFULLY that .45 inch ammunition can be fired in the .455 inch model but .455 inch ammunition may cause serious accidents if an attempt is made to fire it in a .45 inch pistol. This weapon has fixed sights.

STRIPPING.—Take out the magazine and then push in the return spring plunger knurled head which lies underneath the muzzle of the gun and turn the plunger retainer to the left. Take out the plunger retainer return spring and return spring plunger completely. Push the moving part back until the furthermost of the two small gashes on the bottom left edge of the moving part is just over the back end of the long catch on the butt group which is found immediately over the trigger. The long catch has, at its front end, a retainer pin which is fitted through the pistol from one side to the other. Push in the end of the pin projected on the right hand side of the pistol and take off the catch to the left. Then slide to the front from the butt group the moving part of the barrel. which may now be taken off. The positioning pin for the return spring will then fall out of the barrel and can be separated from the moving part by pushing it out at the front. To take off the extractor and firing pin, press the bottom of the firing pin with a nail or punch until the small sliding plate at the rear can be pushed down and taken away, then the spring and firing pin can be taken out and the extractor can also be pulled out backwards.

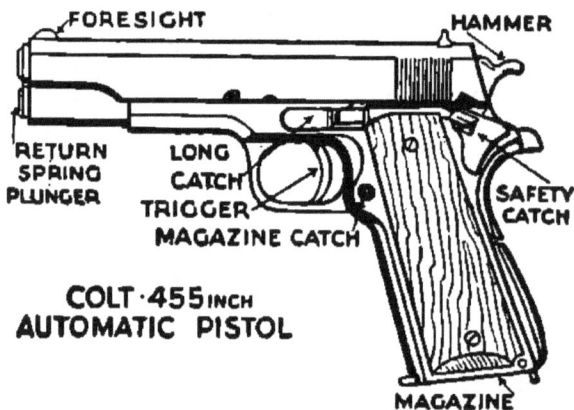

COLT·455ᵢₙcₕ
AUTOMATIC PISTOL

ASSEMBLY.—To re-assemble, reverse the order of the above instructions and make sure to see that, when fitting the long catch pin, it goes through the hole in the barrel link. Always check each assembly operation to see that everything is properly in place.

FILLING THE MAGAZINE.—Remove magazine from the pistol by pushing spring catch that is on the left side of the pistol just behind the trigger, then hold the magazine in the one hand and put the base of each round about half way along the previous one and then press down and backwards by using both your thumbs.

LOADING.—Press the magazine fully home in the butt then press back the moving parts to their fullest extent and allow them to move as far forward as possible. The pistol is now ready to fire.

SAFETY.—For applied safety a catch is fitted on the left hand side of the pistol, which is only appliable when the hammer is in the cocked position—this automatically locks both hammer and trigger. Mechanical safety is ensured by the fact that trigger pressure is not sufficient to release the hammer. The actual pistol must be held in such a manner that the grip that lies under the hammer is pushed forward. Furthermore, the hammer is not releasable until the moving portions are fully to the front and the breech is locked ; this is operated by a small stud in the butt group which is fitted about .25 inch to the front of the hammer. This stud is pressed down by the moving portion passing over it until the breech is locked, then it automatically protrudes again into a cavity on the bottom side of the moving portion. When it is pressed down by the rearward movement of the moving parts, it disconnects the hammer from the trigger so that the former can be cocked by the rearward motion of the recoiling part and only permits re-connection either when released by the removal of the finger pressure on the trigger, or when allowed to rise by the fact that the cavity is just above it.

COLT .38 inch AUTOMATIC PISTOL.

DETAILS.—Length, about 9 inches. Barrel length, including chamber, about 6 inches. Unloaded weight, approximately 2¼ lbs. Fires 7 rounds, using .38 inch rimless ammunition. The loading and unloading details for this pistol are identical with those given previously for the .45 inch Colt Automatic, the only difference being that the magazine catch will be found in the bottom of the butt instead of at the side. All other details are very similar to the previous pistol mentioned and should be followed where they apply.

9 m.m. LUGER AUTOMATIC PISTOL.

This is probably one of the most common of the German automatic pistol that may come into our hands and uses 9 m.m. Parabellum ammunition only. This ammunition can be identified by the fact that it is approximately 1.14 inches to 1.16 inches in length.

DETAILS.—Weight, approximately, 2 lbs. Length, 9 inches. Barrel length, approximately, 4 inches. Holds 8 rounds in a normal magazine.

STRIPPING.—Take off the magazine and slightly press back barrel then move downwards to the vertical position the thumb catch which is found in the front of the trigger guard. Take out the covering plate and pull off to the front the recoiling parts of barrel and receiver. It is advised that no further stripping should be attempted as, in the event of damage being done to any parts, difficulty may be experienced in obtaining spares.

To re-assemble, reverse the above instructions.

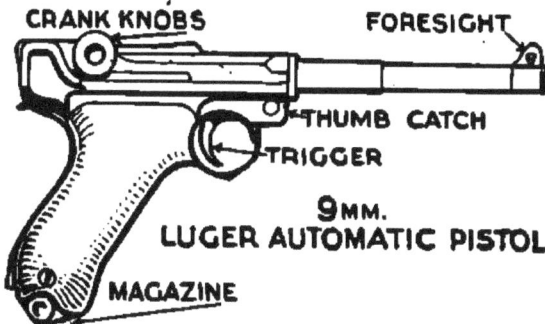

CRANK KNOBS — FORESIGHT — THUMB CATCH — TRIGGER — MAGAZINE

9MM. LUGER AUTOMATIC PISTOL

LOADING.—Fit the mouth of a loaded magazine in the opening at the base of the butt and push it home until the magazine catch is engaged. Push upwards and to the rear with a sharp motion the two knurled knobs on the crank and let go. This will automatically cock the pistol and simultaneously the first round will have been fitted into the firing chamber.

UNLOADING.—Take out by pushing in magazine catch which is found to the rear of the trigger on the left hand side of the pistol, then proceed with the same operation of pulling the crank backwards and let it go. This will automatically extract the round in the firing chamber. Finally, release spring tension by pulling the trigger.

SAFETY.—A safety catch is fitted on the left hand side of the body near the top of the butt. The safety catch can be placed in two positions—the more forward one being the "ready" and the furthest back is the "safe" position. Mechanical safety is ensured by the fact that, if the trigger is pressed when the action is not locked, the trigger bar cannot push in against the sear tail because the latter is then too far to the back owing to the fact that the recoiling portions are not fully forward.

NOTE.—This gun will utilise 9 m.m. sten gun ammunition.

THE MARK I. and II. NORTHOVER PROJECTOR.

This weapon is now being used by many Home Guard units, as it is very effective and of simple design.

DETAILS.—The Northover is a $2\frac{1}{2}$ inches smooth bore gun of breech loading pattern and weighs, in the case of the Mark I., approximately 60 lbs , and in the case of the Mark II., approximately 80 lbs., whilst the Mark I. mounting weighs approximately 75 lbs. and the Mark II. tripod approximately 24 lbs. These weapons were originally designed to fire the self-igniting phosphorus No. 76 Grenade, but they will very effectively also fire the anti-tank grenade and the high explosive No. 36 grenade. An aperture back sight is fitted, having six holes, and a semi-circular hole at the top ; the ranges being 50 to 200 yards in steps of 25 yards. The bottom hole being for the smallest range and the range increasing as the higher holes are used. These sights are graduated for the No. 76 grenade. When using the two other types mentioned above, approximately 50 should be added to this range. The most effective range for all these grenades is approximately 100 yards.

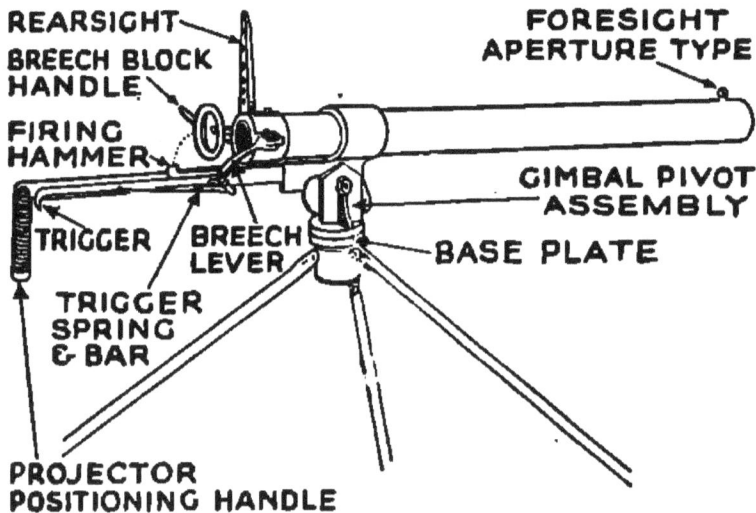

MARK 2 NORTHOVER PROJECTOR

MECHANISM.—A simple type breech mechanism is fitted and consists of a spring locking lever fitted on the left hand side, whilst the breech block itself is hinged on the right hand side. The primer nipple bored through its length fits in the centre of the breech block. The exposed part outside takes the percussion cap and the inner projection, which is formed in the shape of two points, pierces the celluloid powder container of the fire charge so as to permit the flash from the percussion cap to reach the powder when the breech block is after slammed home.

The trigger mechanism has a hammer fitted on to an arm which can move on its axis. The strong spiral spring and the trigger are also used. When the breech block is open the hammer automatically cocks, or it can also be hand cocked if necessary.

FIRING CHARGE.—This consists of two fibre discs and a fibre ring which holds the cylindrical cellophane container which, in its turn, holds approximately 5 drams of black powder. A washer, slightly larger in diameter than the fibre ring holds this in position, whilst at the other end is fitted a disc of spongy rubber. When the breech is slammed home, as explained previously, this celluloid cylinder is automatically pierced so as to allow the percussion cap flash to fire the propellant powder charge. The grenade used in the case of the No. 76 consists of a half-pint bottle which contains a

9 m.m. MAUSER AUTOMATIC PISTOL.

DETAILS.—Length, about 11 inches. Barrel length, approximately, 5 inches. Weight, 2 lbs. 8 ozs. unloaded. Holds 10 rounds and utilizes 9 m.m. Mauser ammunition, which can be identified by the fact that its length is approximately 1⅜ inches. These guns have open sights which are suitable for 50 to 500 metres.

STRIPPING.—Press upwards the stud in the magazine base plate, then move the plate to the fore and take out the magazine platform and spring. Cock the hammer and push up the body catch which is beneath the base of the hammer ; then it is possible to pull to the rear and clear of the body the hammer mechanism, barrel and barrel extension. These three parts can then be easily separated. Make certain when doing so that the body catch does not fall out of the hammer mechanism block. To remove the bolt from the barrel extension, use a penknife blade or small screwdriver to push in the back of the firing pin and give it a 90° turn to the right. The firing pin can then be taken out. Finally, press to the fore the bolt catch on the right side of the barrel extension and pull it out to the right ; this automatically releases the bolt return spring and then allows the bolt to be taken out to the back.

To re-assemble, reverse the above instructions.

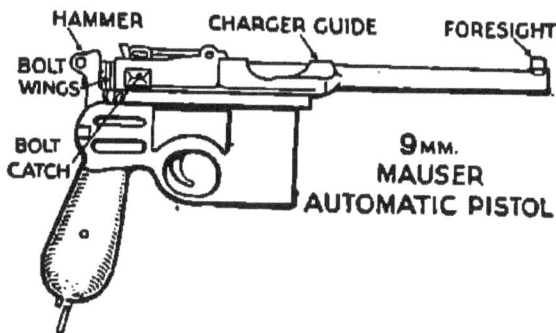

HAMMER   CHARGER GUIDE   FORESIGHT
BOLT WINGS
BOLT CATCH
9 MM. MAUSER AUTOMATIC PISTOL

LOADING.—Pull to the rear the bolt ; this causes the hammer to cock and permits the magazine platform to elevate, at the same time stopping the bolt closing again on an empty breech. Then fit a charger into the guides in the back of the breech and press the rounds into the magazine. Finally, take out the charger and the bolt will then automatically close at the same time moving the first cartridge into the breech ready to fire.

UNLOADING.—Move the bolt to the back and front until it is held open by magazine platform, then hold the bolt back with one hand and push down the magazine platform ; allow the bolt to go forward at the same time, seeing that no round has been left in the breech. Finally, press the trigger.

SAFETY.—The catch is fitted at the side of the hammer on the left of the pistol body. When the catch is in its uppermost position the pistol is at " safety " ; when in a horizontal position, the pistol is cocked and ready for firing.

SPECIAL NOTE.—This make of automatic pistol is also supplied in a 7.63 m.m. model and, to enable the user to distinguish them, all the 9 m.m. patterns are marked with a large " 9 " on each side of the pistol grip.

composition of benzene, latex and phosphorus ; this bottle is shut by means of a metal capsule, coloured green, and must be absolutely air-tight, otherwise the contents will automatically ignite when coming into contact with air. When the grenades are fitted in the projector for firing they are placed in a paper container with a fibre ring at the back end ; this is to prevent breakages whilst firing, as otherwise serious accidents would occur.

When using the No. 36 high explosive grenade a 4-second fuse is fitted and all normal safety measures are carried out. The grenade is fitted without the gas check into the breech of the projector with the base plug end in first. When the grenade is in far enough to hold the striker lever, remove the safety pin and press the grenade fully home.

NOTES.—If a mis-fire takes place fit a new percussion cap and re-cock the hammer by hand. Never open the breech block because some of the actual propellant charge will then fall out. If a No. 76 bottle bursts in the barrel, fire the next round ; this will then clear the previous burst round out. Always make sure that the projectile is back and close up to the propellant powder charge. See that all moving parts are cleaned and oiled and always oil the pivot. Always clean the barrel out with water after firing and, finally, clean by using a ramrod with a .wad fitted at the end. Always make certain that the water being used to clean the barrel is absolutely pure. Paraffin is sometimes very useful for cleaning after many rounds have been fired.

BOYS' ANTI-TANK GUN .55 inch.

DETAILS.—Length, 5 feet 4 inches. Weight, approximately, 35 lbs. Has an overhead box magazine holding five rounds with ejection underneath. Aperture studs are fitted for 300 and 500 yards.

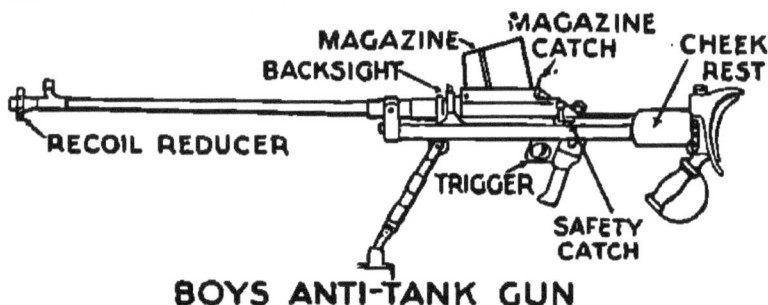

BOYS ANTI-TANK GUN

LOADING & UNLOADING.—The same operations as used for the Bren Gun are utilized in this weapon. For further details of this see our companion volume of " Modern Automatic Guns."

STRIPPING & ASSEMBLY.—To take off the bolt open it and push down the small catch which lies beneath the magazine catch itself ; this enables you to withdraw the bolt. To replace, reverse the above instructions. This gun is a very simple type and the mechanism is virtually the same as the standard service rifle with which most Home Guards are only too well acquainted.

SPECIAL NOTE.—The safety catch is fitted on the left side of the gun and when in the forward position the gun is set for firing, whilst, when the catch is turned to a backward position, the gun is at " safe." Note that this gun has considerable recoil ; therefore, when operating this weapon, always press the right cheek close against the rifle well forward on the cheek rest—making sure that the cheek is clear of the spade grip and shoulder piece so as to prevent possible bruising and broken bones to the firer.

SPECIAL HINTS & TIPS FOR THE PRACTICE & USE OF SMALL ARMS.

MAKING MINIATURE OBJECTS & FIGURES TO CORRECT SCALE FOR USE ON PRACTICE FIRING RANGES.—It is very often necessary to scale down long distance firing due to difficulty in obtaining sufficiently large spaces for practice work, and it is quite easy to actually obtain the same effect on the ordinary small length range. For instance, supposing it is required to illustrate the effect of firing at a 12 feet high object at 750 yards. This can be very easily represented on a 50 yards range by use of the following equation, the result of which gives the size of the object which has to be placed at the end of a 50 yards range so as to obtain the same optical view as though it were at 750 yards distance. First divide the height of the object in feet so as to reduce it to yards, then multiply this by the length of the range in yards, finally dividing the result by the actual length in yards at which the object normally would be at. Thus :—

$$\frac{4 \times 50}{750} = \frac{4}{15} \text{ yards, or approximately } 9\tfrac{3}{4} \text{ inches in height.}$$

In other words, a target having a figure $9\tfrac{3}{4}$ inches in height placed at the end of a 50-yard practice range requires the same accuracy to hit it, as firing at a 12 feet high object at a distance of 750 yards.

TO CALCULATE SPEED OF MOVEMENT SCALED DOWN FOR PRACTICE RANGE USE.—When firing on a short practice range, scaled down objects that are supposed to be moving should move at approximately the correct speed so as to enable the firer to get the best possible type of practice. Let us imagine that it is required to simulate on a 30 yards range a 6-foot man at 1,000 yards distance, and running at a speed of 200 yards a minute. First of all multiply the speed in yards per minute of the moving object by the length of the range, then divide the result by the distance of the object ; this gives the speed in yards per minute at which the object has to move across the actual practice range. Thus :—

$$\frac{200 \times 30}{1,000} = 6 \text{ yards per minute speed of moving object.}$$

Therefore, the object must move across the back of the range at a speed of 6 yards per minute or 3.6 inches per second. To actually calculate the size of the moving object use the equation previously given. Thus :—

$$\frac{2 \times 30}{1,000} = .006 \text{ yards, or approximately 2 inches.}$$

Therefore, to simulate the 6-feet man running at 200 yards per minute at a distance of 1,000 yards on a 30 feet practice range, a figure approximately 2 inches in height moving at a speed of 3.6 inches per second is required.

MARK VI. WEBLEY REVOLVER .455 INCH.

DETAILS.—Service name, No. 1 Pistol. Over-all length, $11\tfrac{1}{4}$ inches. Average barrel length, 6 inches. Weight about $2\tfrac{1}{4}$ lbs. Cylinder turns clockwise. Number of chambers, 6. Uses Mark II. .455 inch lead bullets for practice purposes and Mark VI. .455 inch nickel jacketted ammunition for active service use.

STRIPPING.—Undo screw holding butt grips, then undo trigger guard screws and press the mainspring from out of its seating from the right to left side and unhook the long arm from the hammer swivel. Elevate tail of mainspring auxiliary from out of its seating and take off the auxiliary, then undo hammer axis screw and take off hammer. Remove trigger axis screw and take off trigger and pawl complete. Then undo the holding screw on the cylinder catch and push the bottom of the catch retainer up, thus pressing the back of the catch and allowing the complete removal of cylinder

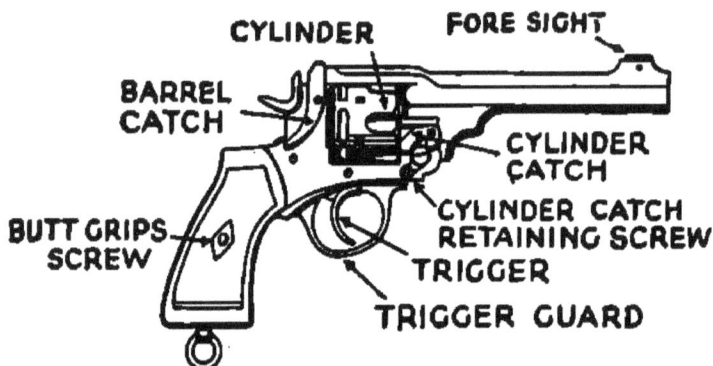

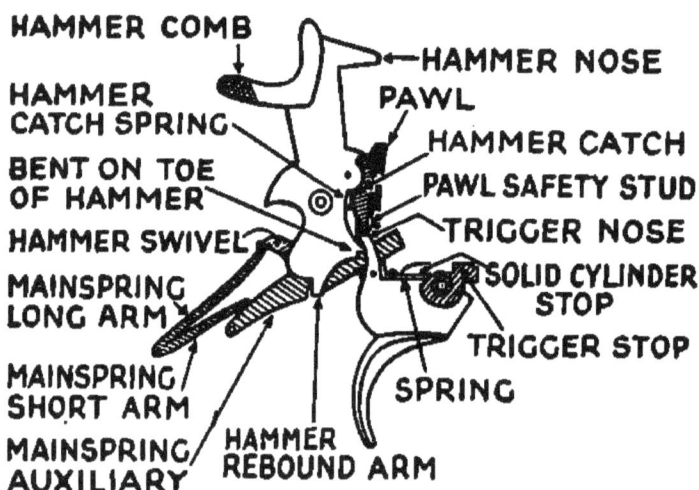

CYLINDER FORE SIGHT

BARREL CATCH

CYLINDER CATCH

CYLINDER CATCH RETAINING SCREW

BUTT GRIPS SCREW

TRIGGER

TRIGGER GUARD

HAMMER COMB

HAMMER NOSE

HAMMER CATCH SPRING

PAWL

HAMMER CATCH

BENT ON TOE OF HAMMER

PAWL SAFETY STUD

HAMMER SWIVEL

TRIGGER NOSE

MAINSPRING LONG ARM

SOLID CYLINDER STOP

MAINSPRING SHORT ARM

TRIGGER STOP

SPRING

MAINSPRING AUXILIARY

HAMMER REBOUND ARM

MARK VI WEBLEY ·455 REVOLVER WITH FULL MECHANISM

ASSEMBLY.—Reverse the order given above and at each stage check for correct functioning and free movement.

MECHANISM—NOTES.—The rotating cylinder is held whilst in the firing position by the pawl, engaging against the ratchet on the cylinder—thus preventing an anti-clockwise motion of the stop on the trigger pressing against the end of one of the slots at the back of the cylinder and preventing it turning too far. Should the revolver be incompletely closed, it is due to the hammer not being able to reach the percussion cap of the " round of ammunition " by the barrel catch, which naturally cannot be properly engaged, otherwise the pistol is so far open that it is impossible for the hammer to reach the percussion cap.

The return of the hammer is obtained by the sloping face of the short side of the mainspring auxiliary pressing against the tail end of the hammer whilst under the influence of the mainspring. Actual mechanical safety is obtained by the hammer tail pressing against the short side of the mainspring auxiliary and, due to this, a blow on the rear of the hammer causes the auxiliary to elevate, and thus the long arm connects with the safety stud on the pawl which forces the pawl to rise. The trigger nose then comes up until it engages against the hammer catch which prevents the hammer moving further—so making it impossible to fire the round.

SMITH & WESSON .455 inch .45 inch D.A. and .38 inch REVOLVERS.

DETAILS.—There are very many varieties of types in these makes as improvements have been constantly taking place, and in war-time many older models are resurrected for service use, due to their still being quite efficient offensive weapons. The main details of all types are as follows :—

All the cylinders have 6 chambers and they always revolve anti-clockwise. The ammunition which is suitable for these various calibres is as follows :—The .45 inch D.A. model uses the automatic .45 inch ammunition which is utilized in the Thompson Sub-Machine carbine ; this is fitted by means of two special 3-round clips. Note that this pistol cannot fire ordinary rimmed ammunition and, furthermore, unless special clips are used, automatic extraction does not operate and each spent case will have to be pressed out individually with a stick or other suitable implement.

The .455 inch utilizes British service or American .455 inch ammunition. Note carefully to see that this is used as, although there is only .005 inch difference in these two types of ammunition, dangerous stoppages and possible accidents can occur by use of the wrong-sized ammunition.

The .38 inch revolver uses any American .38 inch ammunition as long as the cylinder length is over 1¼ inches.

These details should only be taken as general instructions because so many models have appeared of these makes and, if possible, the standard service sheet should be obtained.

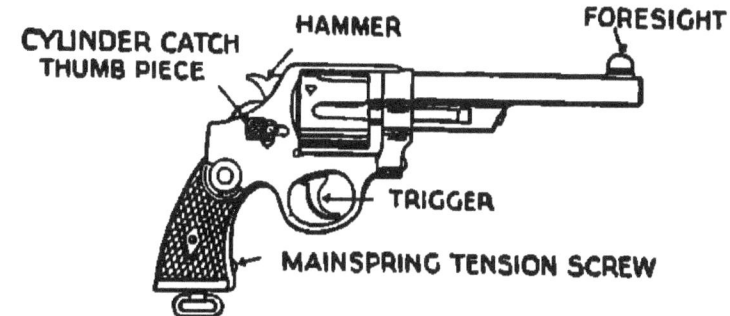

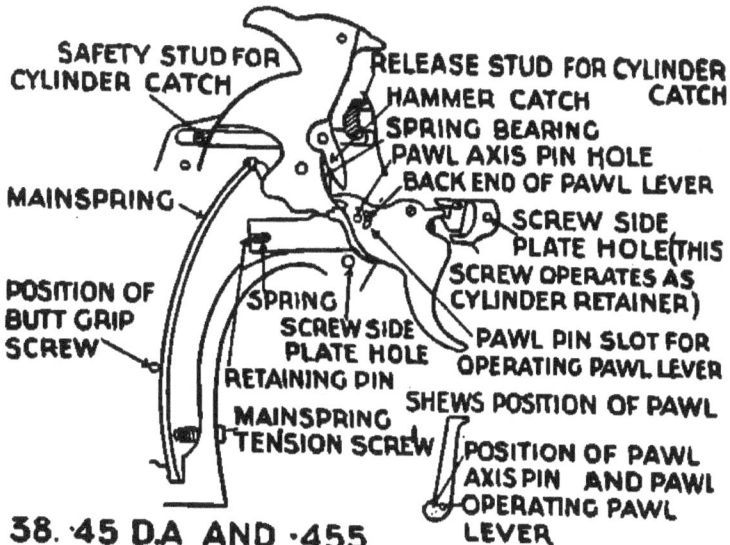

38. 45 D.A AND ·455 SMITH & WESSON REVOLVER WITH MECHANISM

STRIPPING.—Undo the screw holding the butt grips and then undo the four screws which hold the side plate ; this is on the right hand side, whilst in the case of the Colt revolver, it is on the left hand side. Two of these screws are over both ends of the trigger guard and of the other two, one is above the back of the right grip and the other behind the top of the cylinder. Then take off the side plate. Undo tension screw of mainspring which is found at the lower end of the front of the butt frame and take out the mainspring, at the same time undoing it from the arm of the hammer swivel. Press back the pawl so that it disengages from behind the cylinder and take it out with the help of a screwdriver or penknife. Then ease up the rebound stop and spring so as to clear the retaining pin and then take it out—always being careful so as not to allow the actual spring to fly out as it can be quite easily lost. Move the hammer backwards and, by leverage, take it out, then turn trigger forwards and backwards and lever it to the top and take it out. Remove cylinder by pushing the thumb piece to the fore and moving it out leftwards as far as possible, and then pulling it out. Finally, undo the thumb piece screw on the cylinder catch and take out thumb piece cylinder catch and spring complete.

ASSEMBLY.—Refit thumb piece, cylinder catch and screw and press the thumb piece to the back so as to enable the safety stop to clear the hammer. Then refit the hammer. Replace the pawl on to the trigger, making certain that the spring stud on the front of the pawl lever is fitted on the top of the pawl lever spring correctly and that the back of the pawl lever is above the pawl pin operating the pawl lever before fitting the pawl axis pin into its aperture in the base of the trigger nose. Press the hammer to the fore and then refit the pawl and trigger complete, at the same time making certain that the trigger nose lies in between the hammer catch of the bent of the hammer and that the lever of the cylinder stop at the front of the trigger fits in its recess in the cylinder stop and, finally, making sure that the connecting rod of the rebound stop on the trigger does not drop below the trigger guard.

Fit the front end of the rebound stop at the back of the trigger rear and, by means of a penknife, press the rebound stop spring down and manipulate the rebound stop and spring outwards into position at the rear of their retaining pin.

Fit the claws of the mainspring at the rear of the arms of the hammer swivel and then replace the mainspring. Finally, place enough tension on the mainspring so as to retain it in place by means of screwing the mainspring screw home about half way. Refit butt grips and screw, re-screw home mainspring tension screw. Refit cylinder by fitting spindle in its recess and pressing in the spring-supported plunger and then refit the side plate with its four screws.

It should be noted that these details are also applicable for the stripping and assembling of most types of Colt revolvers.

MECHANISM.—The cylinder is held in the firing position by the cylinder catch stud which is itself spring-supported and fits in the centre of the extractor and is held in position in its socket in the body due to the influence of this spring.

Should the cylinder not close properly, the hammer and trigger will not operate due to the interference of the safety stud which is on the back of the cylinder catch release stud ; this is caused by reason of the safety stud entering the cylinder catch stud socket in the body due to the absence of the cylinder catch stud itself. Rebound of the hammer is caused by the rebound stop being moved to the fore due to the action of its spring. The form of the front end of the rebound stop and the hammer rebound arm is such that the forward movement of the rebound stop presses the bottom part of the hammer nose to the back. Mechanical safety is effected by the hammer rebound arm face pressing hard against the upper part of the rebound stop and, thereby, binding. This naturally prevents the hammer nose going to the fore and firing the next round after rebound takes place.

THE WALTHER 9 m.m. AUTOMATIC PISTOL.

This is probably the third most commonly used of German small arms that members of Home Guard units are likely to come across in the event of invasion taking place and, therefore, they should be in a position to understand the use and details of this weapon.

DETAILS.—Approximately 8 inches in length. Barrel length approximately 5 inches, including chamber. Magazine holds 8 rounds and uses 9 m.m. parabellum type of ammunition. Weight about 2¼ lbs. when loaded. This gun is supplied with fixed sights.

STRIPPING.—First make sure that the safety catch is set at "SAFE," then take out the magazine and press back the slide with one hand and lift the "holding open" catch into engagement with the other hand ; rotate the locking lever to the fore as far as possible (the locking lever is fitted on the left hand side of the gun to the fore of the trigger guard). Next, whilst maintaining the slide under hand control, push in the "holding open" catch and move barrel and slide to the fore, then rotate the slide and barrel upside-down and press to the fore a small plunger at the back of the barrel assembly ; this will automatically unlock the locking block and allow the barrel to be separated from the slide. Finally, the locking block can itself be taken from the barrel. Do not try to effect further stripping as the mechanism is liable, in the hands of an inexperienced person, to suffer some possible damage.

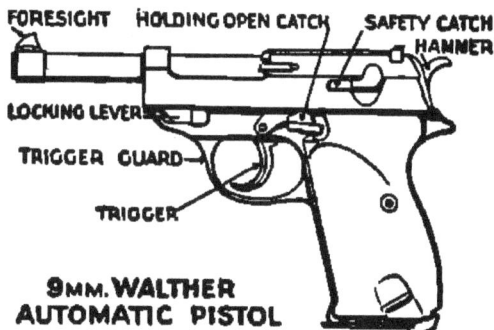

FORESIGHT   HOLDING OPEN CATCH   SAFETY CATCH
HAMMER
LOCKING LEVER
TRIGGER GUARD
TRIGGER

9MM. WALTHER AUTOMATIC PISTOL

ASSEMBLY.—First refit the locking block in the barrel—making sure to see that the lugs on the locking block are truly in line with the barrel. ribs. Then press the barrel assembly into the slide to its furthest extent, press the locking block with an upward motion into the locked position, then note if the hammer is to the fore when the gun is in the un-cocked position, and that all moving parts that are in the body remain beneath the flat bearing surface level at the back end. Place safety catch at "SAFE" and hold locking block in the locked position, then press barrel and slide on to the body, pressing the slide as far back as possible and maintaining it there by lifting the "holding open" catch. Then rotate locking lever to the horizontal or locked position. Finally, push in the "holding open" catch and allow the slide to move to the fore; this will then enable you to insert the magazine.

LOADING.—To remove the magazine, press back catch at the bottom of the pistol grip—this causes the magazine to come out sufficiently far enough to enable it to be held by the fingers and remove. To load the magazine, fit the base of each round to the fore of the magazine lips and push them in a down and backwards motion into place ; then press the magazine back home into the pistol grip and move the slide back to its furthermost extent—finally allowing it to come forward under action of the return spring. It is of no consequence if the safety catch is set at "SAFE" or at the "FIRE" position as, in the former case, the hammer will already be in the firing position, and to actually start firing all that is needed is to set the safety catch at the " FIRE " position and pull the trigger, whilst in the latter case, the weapon is ready cocked and all that is required is to press the trigger. There is no necessity to cock the hammer on this model as a double action hammer mechanism is used which enables the gun to be carried fully loaded but yet be set at " SAFE " with the hammer in an un-cocked position, but it can be ready for action without having to waste time in actually cocking it. The " SAFE " position is when the safety catch is vertically downwards and the " FIRE " position is when the catch is set in the horizontal plane.

UNLOADING.—Take out magazine and move back the slide to its furthermost extent so as to enable the removal of the round from the firing chamber and then allow the slide to move forward. This operation is carried out irrespective of what position the safety catch is in. Should the safety catch be in the " FIRE " position then move it back to " SAFE "—this releases the hammer and removes tension from the springs.

SAFETY MEASURES.—A safety catch is fitted on the left hand side of the gun close to the back end of the slide ; the catch can be moved from the " FIRE " position to the " SAFE " position, irrespective of whether the gun is cocked or un-cocked. Should the pistol be un-cocked, pressing the trigger will not fire the round, due to the fact that the hammer is stopped from moving rearwards sufficiently to be released ; furthermore, the firing pin is automatically locked even if the trigger is not fully retracted. Should the pistol be in the cocked position the hammer will be released and can come to the fore still without firing the round in the chamber because the firing pin is automatically in the locked position prior to the hammer hitting it. It is then automatically impossible to pull the trigger as it is in the fully retracted position.

TRAINING MANUALS, TEXT BOOKS AND INSTRUCTIONS

The backbone of all successful armies is its training and tactics. The Naval and Military Press publishes many such manuals of instruction – all perviously long out of print . So, whether your interest lies in the infantry and cavalry tactics of the earliest regiments of the British army in the 18th century, or the weapons manuals and firing instructions of 20th century warfare, the Naval and Military Press has the right book for you.

www.naval-military-press.com

MINES AND BOOBY TRAPS 1943

This is a War Office pamphlet, issued mid-war, in 1943. Its purpose is to introduce sappers to mines commonly used by the British Army – and how to deal with similar devices set by the Germans. The devices described and illustrated cover British anti-tank; grenade; shrapnel and assorted booby trap switches. Enemy mines are covered in chapter 2 with anti-tank, Teller mine types; French anti-tank; Hungarian; anti-personnel German and Italian; and igniters.This is a concise but comprehensive guide for British Army sappers in the art of demining or mine clearance.

9781474539395

THE .303 LEWIS GUN

Illustrated with good clear line drawings this 1941 weapon guide tells the Home Guard Volunteer how to use the 303 Lewis Gun effectively against the invading enemy.A reprint of an original handbook for the .303 Lewis Gun, that was first published in 1941. This book is a practical guide to the handling and maintenance of this iconic weapon.In the crisis following the Fall of France, where a large part of the British Army's equipment had been lost up to and at Dunkirk, stocks of Lewis guns in both .303 and .30-06 were hurriedly pressed back into service, primarily for Home Guard use. Full of fascinating information, this book taught the user the guns capabilities and all he needed to know about maintenance and combat use. Number 2 in the wartime Nicholson & Watson "Know Your Weapons" series, that offer all the important information in a more vivid style than an official publication. Illustrated with good clear line drawings.

9781474539456

ANTI-TANK WEAPONS
Smash The Tank

An insight into the amateur side of World War 2. Diagrams illustrate the main points and the devices, such as the Thermos Bomb;Phosrhorus Bomb;Sticky Bombs; that could be cobbled together from household items are described.This pamphlet was available to the Home Guard and describes the German tank and how to destroy it. It is an early War publication c1940, dealing with the light tanks used by the Germans, also the author gives examples of anti-tank actions in the Spanish Civil War, in which he took part. I'ts is a fascinating look at the "enthusiastic" approach to killing tanks.

9781474539449

TANK HUNTING AND DESTRUCTION 1940

The stated object for the distributing of this War Office manual was as "A guide and help to troops who have the determination and nerve to destroy tanks at close quarters". Intended for fighting on home soil after the very real possibility of a full German invasion, "Operation Sea Lion", this is a remarkable if somewhat naive snap shot of Britain state of preparedness,in her most dangerous hour.
The contents details Tank hunting, Tank characteristics,Tactical action,Road blocks,ambushes Ect,also includes an interesting appendix on Molotov Cocktails, and materials on other ways to destroy tanks.

9781474539401

TROOP TRAINING FOR LIGHT TANK TROOPS NOVEMBER 1939

Very early War tactics pertaining to various aspects of training with and employing armour in the British Army. Covering in concise detail that which a Light tank crew needed to know to be effective in action.
In the early years of the war, Germany held the initiative. German forces used Blitzkrieg tactics in France in 1940, making full use of the speed and armour of tanks to break through enemy defences. It was clear that German tank tactics had evolved during the inter-war period. By contrast, Britain and the Allies were playing catch-up.

9781474539302

JAPANESE WEAPONS ILLUSTRATED
September 1944

This period 'Restricted' laced binding manual was intended to be an aid to the identification of Japanese Army equipment, with sections covering: Tanks, both two-man, Tankette, light and medium; Armoured Cars; Self-Propelled Guns; Anti-Tank Guns; Artillery; Anti-Aircraft Guns; Mortars & Grenade Dischargers; Small Arms; Flamethrowers etc. Produced one year before the surrender of Japan, this work gives a good overview of the weapons the allies would find, fighting an army that despite being on the back foot, was still capable of stiff resistance in an almost entirely defensive role..

9781474539432

NOTES ON THE GERMAN ARMY-WAR
December 1940

An early war 393-page 'Notes' periodical manual from December 1940. It is a detailed review, for use in the field. The manual looks at every aspect of the "Blitzkrieg" German Army (and, to some extent, the Air Force) and gives details as known at the time.

It covers the fighting arms and the services behind them – tactics, organisation, weapons and equipment. It usefully also includes a colour section on uniforms and insignia, a black-and-white plate section of small arms, infantry support and anti-tank weapons, artillery and AFVs. A series of pull-outs related to the text covering tanks etc. are also reproduced.

This is an important first-class picture of the complex fighting machine that was the German Army at the end of the campaigns of 1940, only six months before the invasion of Russia.

9781474539203

GERMAN MINES AND TRAPS

Mid-1940 War Office manual with details of German mines, both the Teller and S-mine (Bouncing Betty) are covered, with techniques for disarming. Good clear full-page line drawings give both practical and technical information. Highly recommended because of the illustrations, which show how these devices worked and the components.

9781474535809

NOTES ON ENEMY ARMY IDENTIFICATIONS ITALY
October 1941

This period handbook was published to give British military personnel a better understanding of the principal characteristics of both the Italian army and the Black Shirt Militia under active service conditions , it is dated October 1941.

It begins with a description of distinctive branches, or specialities, the most characteristic of which was the arm of the Royal Carabinieri, a semi-military body occupying, historically, the senior position in the Army. Other specialities included the Grenadiers of Sardinia, the Bersaglieri, the Alpini and the San Marco Marine Regiment

The handbook then goes on to show, in order, the organisation of Command and Staff, of formations (corps and divisions) and of the arms and services; services, supply and transportation; ranks, plates (many in colour) cover uniforms, insignia, medals and decorations; armament and equipment and a chapter on the Air Force, There are chapters on tactical doctrine and principles of employment, on permanent fortifications, camouflage and abbreviations. Finally there is a brief index.

9781474539746

MANUAL OF GUERILLA TACTICS
Specially Prepared And Based On Lessons From
The Spanish And Russian Campaigns

One of the excellent, concise Bernards Pocket Books, intended to show members of the Home Guard and the regular forces that war is not conducted in a gentlemanly way – it is kill or be killed.

9781474539463

THE OFFENSIVE OF SMALL UNITS
September 1916

This is a periodical tactical manual from 1916, it focuses on the manner in which the French organised and executed their attacks and counterattacks . Summarised from the French, it lays out the process by which to operate in attacks on the German trenches. Focused purely on the operation of infantry, the purpose of this British translation is to give small infantry units the benefit of the French experience in regard to the best methods of combat, in offensive operations.

9781474537971

TRENCH WARFARE
Notes on attack and defence, February 1915

This important period manual was published in early 1915 when hope of a quick ending to the war disappeared, and trench warfare had begun to dominate the Western Front.

The manual strives to instil an offensive spirit and gives practical examples on: Close quarter, local, methods of successful warfare, and German attacks. The salient points to gather were preparation and co-operation between artillery and infantry, and that the capture of trenches is easier than their retention. Two plates illustrating tactics complete this official publication.

9781474539807

Ministry Of Home Security
OBJECTS DROPPED FROM THE AIR 1941

An illustrated Official and confidential publication, covering the many and varied types of objects that were falling from principally German aircraft during the Second phase of the blitz, including high explosives,incendiary bombs and small arms ammunition. Complete with 8 page addendum.

9781783319541

THE MUSKETRY INSTRUCTIONS
FOR THE GERMAN INFANTRY 1887
(Schiessvorshrift fur die Infanterie)
Translated for the intelligence Division War Office

Translated for the War Office by Colonel C W Bowdler Bell

A facsimile that includes the supplement for the German Infantry for 1887. Musketry exercises were intended to give the infantry instruction in shooting, to make effective use of their firearm in battle. As such the manual shows important details designed to make the infantry soldier battle-ready by the end of his first year of service. Instruction is subdivided into Preparatory exercises; Target practice; Field firing; Instructional firing; Inspection in musketry; Proving the rifle M/61.84 and revolver M/83. Many black powder weapons were still used, mainly for training purposes, up to end of the First World War.

9781783313631